CLOCKS

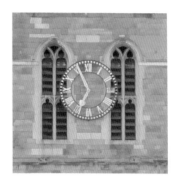

Front cover The Royal Courts of Justice, Strand, WC2
Overleaf Southwark Cathedral, SE1
Opposite London Bridge station, SE1
Back cover St Pancras station, N1

Acknowledgements
My thanks to my research assistant Ruth Sliwinski and the
many clock designers who made this book possible.

ISBN 978-1-85414-373-0

First published 2013

Published by Capital History Publishing
www.capitalhistory.com

Printed by Parksons Graphics

London Clocks

CAPITAL HISTORY

INTRODUCTION

My interest in clocks goes back to an early age when, out of curiosity, I dismantled to the smallest component the family's alarm clock. We were not a rich family and, as no-one could put it back together, a new one was bought using money set aside for my birthday and the dismantled clock became my present. I was more than happy with this and set myself the task of reassembling it – something, with patience and determination, I was able to complete. It was a proud achievement, marred only by the fact that it never worked again.

The oldest clock in this album of central London clocks is the one at Westminster Abbey, which is of a design that pre-dates the use of a minute hand and is of a pattern from 1745. The minute hand did not appear on clocks until the late 18th century, hence expressions like half past seven rather than the more precise-sounding 7.30 - or the even more precise-sounding (because of its use in the military and in railway timetables) 0730 hours. You may ask how it is that the clock at St James Garlickhythe has the date 1682 when it has two hands; likewise the clock at St Andrew Holborn which shows the year 1752. The former is the date the church was built after the Great Fire of London, not the date of the clock. The latter is clearly a modern clock carrying an earlier date; not uncommon. Dating clocks has many pitfalls so the years that sometimes appear on clocks cannot be relied upon to indicate when the clock, or even any clock, was installed. Many clocks that look old are in fact modern replicas or different designs from the originals; e.g. the 2004 clock (page 89) on the former church in Old Street that is now the LSO rehearsal rooms or those at St Pancras on the back cover (2007).

Another example is the famous Selfridges clock. As it fits so well with the rest of the building I had assumed it was there from the start; however it actually dates from the store's twenty-fifth anniversary year, 1931. The ornate clock above the main entrance of Fortnum & Mason is also rather more recent that it looks, dating from 1964. Clocks are sometimes threatened when a building changes ownership. A number were lost when newspaper production moved from the Fleet Street area in the 1980s; one that survived was the impressive 1928 clock on the former Daily Telegraph building (page 13). Indeed Fleet Street has a number of interesting clocks, not least of which is the splendid one on the 1882 Royal Courts of Justice (front cover). The smallest clock in this book is the one on page 76, a modern clock included solely because of the 1900 case in which it is housed. The largest clock face in the book – indeed the largest in central London – is the one on the Shell Mex building (page 17), which dates from 1930. Not all clocks in this book are in working order, but most are. Enjoy them, but check your watch! Some show the correct time only 730 times a year, or 732 times in a leap year.

James Whiting

NO MINUTE GONE COMES EVER BACK AGAIN TAKE HEED AND SEE YE NOTHING DO IN VAIN

VT PROSIM

'Big Ben', SW1 ➤

28 Lexington Street, W1 ➤

EST. 1749

TIFFANY & CO.

187 FLEET STREET

Holy Trinity Church, Marylebone Road, NW1

1682

1863

Car park

Great Western
First Class Lounge

Hammersmith & City lin
Circle line via King's Cro

19 Eastbourne Terrac

Toilets

Self service ticke